KT-425-429

COUNTY LIBRARY
WITHDRAWN
SCHOOLS LIBRARY &
RESOURCES SERVICE

2100007710

E.L.R.S.

SPOTLIGHT ON
THE
INTER-WAR
YEARS

Michael Gibson

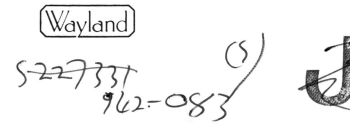

S-227331 (S)
962-083

SPOTLIGHT ON HISTORY

Cover Illustration: Summer Afternoon Tea, from a French fashion magazine, 1924

First published in 1986 by Wayland (Publishers) Ltd
61 Western Road, Hove, East Sussex, BN3 1JD, England

© Copyright 1986 Wayland (Publishers) Ltd

British Library Cataloguing in Publication Data
Gibson, Michael, *1936*
Spotlight on the Inter-War Years
(Spotlight on history)
1. History, Modern—20th Century—Juvenile
literature
I. Title 909.82′2   D422

ISBN 0-85078-973-7

Printed in Great Britain at The Bath Press, Avon

CONTENTS

1 'A BRAVE NEW WORLD'

When the First World War ended on 11 November 1918, 13,000,000 men had been killed leaving 10,000,000 widows and orphans. The amount of money spent on the war could have provided a home and land for every family in Britain, France, Germany, Russia, the United States, Canada and Australia.

The peacemakers

The task facing the peacemakers at the Versailles Conference in 1919 was formidable. President Wilson of the United States and Prime Minister Lloyd George of Britain could afford to be generous to their enemies but 'Tiger' Clemenceau, the Premier of France, was determined to destroy Germany for ever. Orlando, the Prime Minister of Italy, needed to obtain major territorial gains for his country if he was to stay in power. The peace treaties that emerged from months of argument were harsh, but not as savage as the Treaty of

On 19 November 1918, the Armistice was signed in Marshal Foch's railway coach headquarters, in a siding near Compiégne, in France.

Left to right, the leaders – Lloyd George, Orlando, Clemenceau and Wilson have a friendly discussion during the talks at the Peace Conference in Versailles, 1919.

Brest-Litovsk, which the Germans had forced the defeated Russians to accept in March 1918.

The Treaty of Versailles
By the Treaty of Versailles, which was signed on 28 June 1919, Germany was stripped of her overseas empire. She lost the gains she had made by the Treaty of Brest-Litovsk and part of eastern Prussia (the Polish Corridor). Alsace and Lorraine were returned to France and the Saar, a rich mining and industrial area, was placed under League of Nations control. The Rhinelands were occupied by French and British troops. Germany had to surrender her Grand Fleet, disband her air force and reduce her army to a paltry 200,000 men. In addition, the Reparations Commission decided she was to pay £7,000 million compensation to the victorious Allies. Worse still, Germany was forced by threat of military occupation to accept the treaty—the *diktat* or 'dictated treaty' as the Germans called it – and its infamous War Guilt Clause: 'The Allied Governments affirm and Germany accepts the responsibility of Germany and her allies for causing all the loss and damage, to which the Allied Governments and their nationals have been subjected, as a consequence of the war imposed upon them by the aggression of Germany and her allies.' The Germans deeply resented this and were determined to wipe out this insult to their national honour.

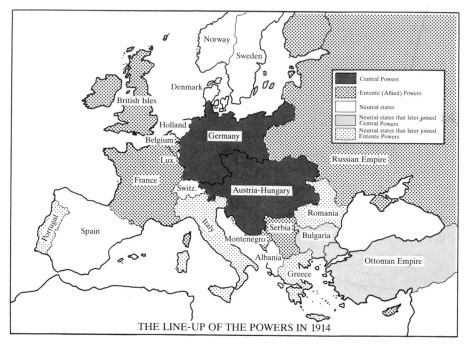

THE LINE-UP OF THE POWERS IN 1914

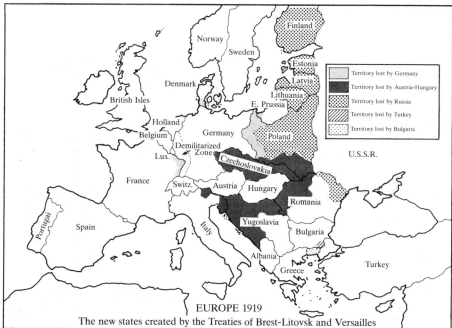

EUROPE 1919

The new states created by the Treaties of Brest-Litovsk and Versailles

The map of Europe after the 1914–1918 War. By the Treaty of Versailles, Germany lost Alsace-Lorraine, Upper Silesia and her overseas empire.

The new states

The other treaties were just as harsh. As a result of the Treaty of St Germains, the Austro-Hungarian Empire was divided into Austria, Hungary, Czechoslovakia and Jugoslavia (now Yugoslavia). None of these new countries had strong economies or defences and they all contained restive minority groups who threatened their peace. By the Treaty of Neuilly, Bulgaria ceded her possessions in Thrace to Greece. The Treaty of Sèvres in 1919 failed to solve the Turkish question, but the Treaty of Lausanne, in 1923, succeeded. The new republic of Turkey ceded her part of Thrace to Greece, gave up her overseas empire and agreed to the neutralization of the straits which separate the Black Sea from the Mediterranean. The map of Europe had been redrawn. Many old problems had been solved but many new ones appeared to take their place.

The League of Nations

Most Europeans hoped the League of Nations assembly, a kind of parliament (with the aim of preserving world peace), would succeed in changing the way nations acted. However, the League was crippled by weaknesses from the beginning. It was a severe blow that the United States, the most powerful country on earth, refused to join. Moreover,

The first Session of the League of Nations in 1920 at the Hague.

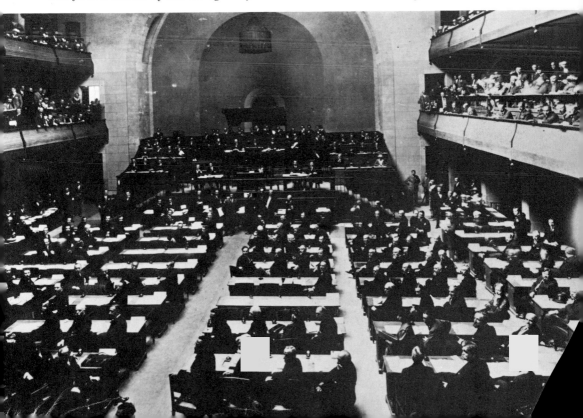

the League had no means of enforcing disarmament which was the key to world peace. Even worse, it had no armed force with which to defend its members against aggressors. According to Lenin, the Russian Bolshevik leader, 'The League is a "robbers' den" to safeguard the unjust spoils of Versailles.'

Everything went wrong during the immediate post-war period. Europe was badly hit by a severe slump in trade. In 1923, the French occupied the Ruhr, a great German industrial district, when the Germans could not meet their reparations payments. This increased German resentment. Although the Dawes (1924) and Young (1929) plans reduced the size of Germany's liability and made her annual reparations payments more realistic, the harm had been done. Germany had been humiliated and many of her people had lost their savings.

Reconciliation

The Locarno Treaties of 1925 seemed a big step towards reconciliation. France, Belgium and Germany guaranteed Germany's western borders; while Poland, Czechoslovakia and Germany guaranteed her eastern frontiers. In 1926, Germany entered the League of Nations and, on the surface at least, all seemed well. There was even a conference in Geneva in 1927 on naval disarmament. Post-war optimism reached its height in 1928 when representatives from most countries in the world signed the Kellogg-Briand Pact condemning war. During 1929–30 the hated Franco-British armies of occupation withdrew from the German Rhinelands.

A victim of the plunging stock prices during the Wall Street Crash, New York, October 1929, tries to raise money.

29 February 1932, the Thames jammed with ships in an attempt to unload their cargoes before the introduction of new customs duties on foreign goods.

The economic whirlwind

We will never know whether the wounds inflicted by the First World War and the peace treaties would have healed had there been a lengthy period of peace and affluence, because in 1929 the Wall Street Crash changed the whole scene. The United States had been enjoying an artificial boom for years. Suddenly, on 23 October 1929, speculators lost confidence in the American economy and millions of shares changed hands at knock-down prices. In the ensuing panic, the United States called in its loans to foreign countries.

At this time, the United States controlled the world economy. As the leading commentator J. M. Keynes put it, 'The United States lends money to Germany, Germany transfers its equivalent as reparations to the Allies, the Allies pass it back to the United States Government.' As long as this process continued, all was well, but as soon as the United States stopped making loans, Germany and her wartime allies were unable to make their reparations payments. As a result, the Allies could not repay the United States the debts they owed her. World trade almost collapsed and every country took steps to save its own economy by imposing customs duties to exclude foreign goods. This hit the manufacturing nations particularly hard and led to large-scale unemployment.

Each nation blamed its neighbours for the situation. In this atmosphere of fear and hardship, the wounds inflicted by the First World War and the peace treaties opened once more.

13

WEST GLAMORGAN COUNTY LIBRARIES

2 BRITAIN BETWEEN THE WARS

The First World War shattered Britain's claim to be the greatest power in the world. By 1918, she had sold £2,000 million worth of overseas investments, she had lost many of her markets and owed the United States a large debt. The Prime Minister, Lloyd George, persuaded the Conservatives to continue their support for his Liberals and took advantage of his popularity by holding a snap election in 1919, which he won by promising to make Germany pay for the war.

Post-war problems

The immediate post-war period witnessed severe industrial troubles. Most trade unionists wanted British industry to be nationalized. In 1921, when the government refused to meet the miners' demands, they went on strike, but were defeated. The post-war slump forced the government to reduce expenditure on the armed forces by using

Striking miners in Britain after the government refused to meet their demands in 1921.

Ramsay MacDonald on his way to form the first Labour Government in 1924.

the 'Geddes axe' (reforms in the economy named after the chairman of the committee on national expenditure). By 1922, Lloyd George, 'the little Welsh Wizard', was thoroughly unpopular and his coalition government broke up. In the subsequent election the Conservatives won an overwhelming victory and Bonar Law became Prime Minister until ill health forced him to resign. His place was taken by Stanley Baldwin, who tried to persuade the electorate that Britain should reintroduce customs duties to protect industry. As a result the Conservatives were defeated in the election of December 1923. To the horror of much of the country Ramsay MacDonald formed Britain's first Labour Government in January 1924.

The first Labour Government
Although the Labour ministry was short-lived, it gave promise of better things to come. The Wheatley Housing Act, for example, eventually provided 500,000 houses. The National Insurance Act made benefit continuous instead of intermittent. Abroad, MacDonald made a good impression. He helped to get the Dawes Plan accepted, negotiated a trade agreement with Russia and drew up the Geneva Protocol for the permanent settlement of international disputes. The government fell as a result of the 'Red Scare'. The newspapers published the text of the 'Zinoviev Letter'. This was a fake 'Russian plan' outlining preparations for a revolution in Britain.

Protest marches during the General Strike of 1926.

The General Strike

On being restored to power, Baldwin and the Conservatives (1925–9) returned to the gold standard causing the price of British exports to rise. British industrialists sought to reduce wage levels to make their goods more competitive. The miners refused to consider wage reductions and on 'Red Friday', 31 June 1925, the government agreed to subsidize their wages while the Samuel Commission studied their situation. Neither the mine-owners nor their employees, however, would accept the commission's recommendations and the General Strike took place between 3 and 12 May 1926. As a contemporary observed, 'For some it was just a game. As I took my ticket home on the bus, the conductor said, "Fraid you'll have to drive this thing yourself tomorrow, sir." And sure enough, next morning, the tremendous upper-middle class lark began.' In some areas, the strikers and the police played friendly football matches. In others, the peace was kept by armoured cars patrolling the streets. The strike collapsed in nine days. The miners were defeated and the membership of the trade union movement slumped.

The National Government

In 1929, MacDonald and the Labour Party won the general election and formed their second ministry. Almost immediately the country felt the effects of the Wall Street Crash. By 1931, panic was spreading and King George V asked MacDonald to form a National Government with the Conservatives and Liberals to deal with the economic crisis. Many members of the Labour party were furious and withdrew their support. Although the National Government protected British industry by placing import duties on foreign goods, unemployment remained high. In South Wales, 'the sight was one of the most doleful I have ever seen in my life,' reported a contemporary. 'It consisted chiefly of this: (unemployed) men . . . standing with their hands in their pockets along the street kerb . . . I knew that if I asked some of them, they would tell me they were "waiting for something to pass by"—a chance to run an errand, or do something to earn a few pence. Others, especially the men over thirty-five . . . would answer they were waiting for the Old Age Pension to come along.'

Ramsay MacDonald (bottom row centre) with members of his Cabinet in 1929.

The Depression

During the Depression there were between twelve and fifteen million unemployed in the United States, six million in Germany until Hitler came to power, and almost three million in Britain. This meant wounded pride for the men and poverty for their families.

An unemployed man in Britain with a wife and children received about £1.50 a week, barely enough to feed them. There was no spare cash for luxuries such as clothes or recreation. It is possible that a quarter of the nation was badly clothed, underfed and living in appalling conditions in many industrial areas. 'In Manchester,' it was observed, 'practically all the houses in the slum belt, numbering about 80,000, will have to be demolished and replaced by modern houses and flats.' Britain was divided into two countries: the relatively well-off south and the poverty-stricken north.

An example of the appalling conditions in the north of England in 1933.

Edward VIII (second from right) gave up the throne so that he was free to marry Mrs Wallis Simpson.

The Abdication crisis

While the government grappled unsuccessfully with unemployment, there was a royal crisis. When George V died in 1936, most people expected his son, Edward VIII, to reign for many years. To the dismay and astonishment of his people, it became known that he wished to marry a twice-divorced American lady called Mrs Wallis Simpson. The governments of the British Commonwealth nations were opposed to the marriage and on 11 December 1936, the King announced, 'I have found it impossible to carry the heavy burden and responsibility and to discharge my duties as King as I would wish to do without the help and support of the woman I love.' He abdicated and was replaced by his brother George VI, whose coronation was celebrated in 1937.

The new Britain

The twenties and thirties saw revolutionary changes in British society. The aristocracy was hard hit and complained, 'large estates . . . have been and are still being broken up, and the houses attached to them, sold to individuals most of whom have had little or no connection with the land.' This new Britain consisted 'of arterial and by-pass roads, of filling stations and factories that look like exhibition buildings, of great cinemas and dance halls and cafés, bungalows with tiny garages, cocktail bars, Woolworths, motor-coaches, wireless, hiking, factory girls looking like actresses, greyhound racing, and dirt tracks, swimming, and everything given away for cigarette coupons.' George Orwell, the famous novelist, pointed out the irony of the situation: 'Twenty million people are underfed but literally everyone in England has access to a radio.'

Older people were shocked by the social changes, particularly those in young women's behaviour. As one critic snarled in the twenties, 'Supposedly "nice girls" were openly smoking cigarettes—openly defiantly, if often awkwardly and self-consciously. They were drinking ... Worse still, they were starting to paint their faces.' A poet put the following words into their mouths:

> We've silken legs and scarlet lips
> We're young and hungry, wild and free,
> Our waists are round about the hips,
> Our skirts are well above the knee.

The Britain that entered the Second World War in 1939 had few of the characteristics it showed in 1914.

In spite of the upheaval of Edward VIII's abdication the British people welcomed the coronation of his brother George VI, in May 1937.

3 FRANCE AND SPAIN

France's post-war problems

France suffered terribly during the First World War. The industrial and mining north was devastated, well over a million men were killed and she was practically bankrupt. Taxes were raised but still the government could not pay the country's bills. The French declared angrily, 'We won the war but lost the peace.' When a general election was held, the Bloc National consisting of right-wing Conservatives led by Poincaré won. However, their support soon fell away when they failed to obtain large cash payments from Germany and had to face a severe post-war slump. The unsuccessful occupation of the Ruhr in 1923 led to the government's defeat in the following year by a coalition of Radicals and Socialists called the Cartel des Gauches.

The new coalition was no more successful than its predecessor. At home, old wounds were opened when the government tried to break the power of the Roman Catholic Church in the newly regained provinces of Alsace and Lorraine. This policy not only failed but created

A memorial to those Frenchmen lost during the First World War.

lasting ill-will. In Morocco, Abdul Krim and his savage tribesmen rose in revolt and government forces had to conduct a bloody war in the mountains. Finally, the value of the franc plummeted from seventy to the pound in 1924 to 250 to the pound in 1926. The government fell and Poincaré returned to power at the head of the right-wing Union Nationale.

The Stavisky affair

For a time the new government ruled by emergency decree. As soon as the franc had been saved, however, the coalition broke up and Aristide Briand took over as Premier. Almost immediately France was overwhelmed by the Great Depression following the Wall Street Crash. Between the collapse of Union Nationale in December 1932 and February 1934 there were four different governments. During this period of instability, France was rocked by the Stavisky scandal. Stavisky, a crooked financier, was found dead, silenced, many people believed, by corrupt politicians who had made use of his services. During this crisis, riots took place in Paris and eleven people were killed and 300 injured. A new Union Nationale government weathered the storm.

Between 1932 and 1934 France suffered a period of great instability and there were many demonstrations and riots.

*The French demonstrate the strength of a gun emplacement in the
Maginot line which separated France from Germany.*

The rearmament debate

In 1936, Leon Blum formed a Popular Front government which did
a great deal of good: wages were raised, holidays with pay provided
and the working week reduced to forty hours. However, the country
was dissatisfied as the French economy remained weak and there were
outbreaks of violence between the French Fascists, the Croix de Feu,
and the Communists. In 1937 the government broke up and Daladier
took over. Rearmament became the main talking point. Colonel
Charles de Gaulle (a future leader of France), proposed the creation
'as a matter of urgency of an army of manoeuvre and attack, mecha-
nized, armoured, composed of picked men.' The French, however,
preferred to place their trust in a great concrete wall called the Maginot
Line which separated them from Germany. The wall was built during
1929–36 under the direction of the War Minister, André Maginot; it
consisted of semi-underground forts armed with heavy guns, joined
by underground passages, and protected by anti-tank defences. As
Paul Reynaud wrote, 'If war broke out, concrete would take the place
of bodies; we would no longer be exposing young Frenchmen to the
perils of an offensive.' Memories of the terrible First World War battles
were still very much alive.

General Franco (centre), the leader of the right-wing Nationalists, confers with his colleagues.

Anarchy in Spain

Even though Spain remained neutral during the First World War, her people were deeply unhappy. The country was poor, backward and deeply divided politically. In 1928, General Primo de Rivera overthrew the democratic government and set up a right-wing dictatorship. When he fell from power in 1930, democracy was restored. The following year, however, King Alphonso fled and a republic was established with left-wing support.

From the beginning, right-wing Nationalist politicians, especially the Falange Española, consisting largely of army officers and university students, hated the republic. As Gil Robles, a leading commentator, pointed out: 'A country can live under a monarchy or a republic, with a parliamentary or a presidential system, under Communism or Fascism. But it cannot live in anarchy ... we are today present at the funeral service of a democracy.' When left-wing parties won the 1936 election, civil war broke out.

The Civil War

Right-wing Nationalists led by General Francisco Franco were supported by most of the armed forces and the Roman Catholic Church. They also received help from Hitler and Mussolini. The left-wing

Republicans obtained aid from the Soviet Union, and from the International Brigade which was made up of volunteers from all over the world. Britain and France were the only major European powers to observe strict neutrality.

The war was fought with great ferocity. When told that half Spain was Communist, General Queipo de Llano replied, 'Very well, we shall exterminate half Spain.' Both sides used terrible brutality. After the massacre of the inhabitants of Badajoz in 1936, an eyewitness wrote, 'Blood had poured in streams from the pavement. Everywhere you found clotted pools.' In spite of the Republicans' determined resistance, the Nationalists surrounded Madrid, the capital. The city became a battlefield. At the university, 'the light shone through shell holes in the walls, from the windows the shattered sunblinds hung drunkenly awry, a wrecked car sprawled in the drive, and there were great holes in the ground full of water.' The air-raids were so frightening that 'people prayed for rain and bad weather to keep the bombers grounded.'

Many Spanish cities suffered terrible devastation during the Civil War.

Picasso's famous painting Guernica, depicting the horror of the Spanish Civil War.

The tragedy of Guernica

The war dragged on until March 1939 when Madrid fell to Franco. Although the fighting had brought devastation to great areas of Spain, one atrocity above all others lived in the memories of Europeans—the tragedy of Guernica. Guernica was a small town with 7,000 inhabitants in the Basque province of Viscaya. At half past four on 26 April 1937, planes started to bomb and machine-gun the town. Within an hour, it had been reduced to rubble. Large numbers of people were killed or wounded. This was the work of the infamous Nazi Condor squadron. Later, Hermann Goering, Hitler's second-in-command and the chief of the *Luftwaffe* (the German air force), admitted that the attack on Guernica was an experiment to try out the new *blitzkrieg* tactics (swift, shattering campaigns, literally meaning in German 'lightning war').

Man's inhumanity to man

Not long after the tragedy, Pablo Picasso was commissioned to paint a mural for the Spanish Government building at the World Fair in Paris. He chose as his subject the horrors of war as expressed by the destruction of Guernica—the painting is generally regarded as a masterpiece. The Nationalist General in charge of the Basque campaign boasted, 'I have decided to terminate rapidly the war in the north. If they (the Republicans) do not surrender immediately, I will raze all Vizcaya to the ground.' Little did he know that his ill-omened words would be realized almost immediately and that this action would become the symbol of man's inhumanity to man.

4 THE NEW ROMAN EMPIRE

The Italians were angered and frustrated by the peace treaties. Many felt they had been tricked into entering the First World War by the Allies' big promises. In return for their great economic and human sacrifices, they only received the South Tyrol and Istria.

Gabriele D'Annunzio, a Nationalist, seized the opportunity presented by growing disorder to occupy Fiume in Jugoslavia. Giolitti, the Italian Prime Minister, had to order the army to remove the people's hero. In this situation, most Italians became attracted by extremist politicians. On the right, there were the *Fasci di Combattimento*, created by Benito Mussolini in 1919. On the left were the Communists. Pitched battles took place between the two.

Mussolini's Fascist supporters in Rome, 1922.

Mussolini and King Victor Emmanuel inspect a parade.

The March on Rome

Although the Fascists only gained thirty-five out of 535 seats in the Italian parliament in 1921, Mussolini's star was rising. In the chaos resulting from the post-war slump, Giolitti resigned and Mussolini boasted: 'I assure you in all solemnity that the hour has struck. Either they give us the government or we shall take it by falling on Rome.' Sporadic fighting broke out but King Victor Emmanuel refused to use the army to restore peace. When the Fascists prepared to make their threatened 'March on Rome' (most went by train), the King invited Mussolini to form a government.

The murder of Matteotti

Because his party only had a small minority of the seats in parliament, Mussolini ruled at first with a mixture of legality and violence. People who dared to criticize the Fascists were brutally attacked by the notorious Blackshirts. 'If you met them in the street in daytime,' wrote an eyewitness, 'they would be humble and fawning. By night and in numbers they were wicked and evil.' Mussolini's ruthlessness was demonstrated by the murder of the Socialist Deputy, Matteotti, who openly attacked his government. Matteotti disappeared and then his 'body was found naked and contorted, with a pointed file in the breast.' A wave of anger greeted the news of this outrage and Mussolini was in danger of losing control. However, he was a great orator and actor and told the Italian parliament, 'I declare before this assembly and before the Italian people that I alone assume the moral, political and historical responsibility for all that has taken place.'

The Exceptional Decrees

A number of attempts on Mussolini's life during 1925 gave him the opportunity to set up a dictatorship. On 31 October 1926, he passed the Exceptional Decrees which suppressed all but the Fascist party, closed down all anti-Fascist newspapers, abolished the masonic movement, set up special tribunals to try political prisoners and instituted the death penalty for those who attempted to assassinate either the king or himself. The Chief of the Police, Arturo Bocchini, was one of his main supporters. The UPI, a special investigatory department, was set up to discover critics whom the OVRA, or political police, hunted down and killed. The Roselli brothers, the leaders of Justice and Liberty, the main anti-Fascist movement, were tracked down and assassinated in France in 1937.

Although the constitution, king, cabinet and parliament were retained, they ceased to have any importance. Mussolini was *Il Duce*, the Leader, and ruled absolutely through the Fascist Grand Council.

This Fascist propaganda cartoon shows a child being encouraged to think of Mussolini as a benevolent 'father'.

BENITO MUSSOLINI
ama molto i bambini.
I bimbi d'Italia amano
molto il Duce.

VIVA IL DUCE!

Saluto al Duce:

A noi!

29

The newspapers, books, films and the radio were all censored. Local government was carried out by Fascist officials. Schools and universities were brought under State control. Teachers had to wear uniform and use specially written Fascist textbooks. Fascist youth organizations provided political education as well as recreational pursuits.

Mussolini realized that he could not afford to quarrel with the Roman Catholic Church and managed to negotiate the Concordat of 1929. By this agreement, the Pope recognized the Kingdom of Italy, while Italy accepted the Pope as the head of the tiny Vatican State inside the city of Rome. As a result Mussolini achieved an uneasy peace with the Church.

The Corporative State

Mussolini dreamt of revolutionizing the Italian economy by creating a 'corporative state'. The employers and employees of every industry were formed into 'National Confederations'. Strikes and lock-outs were forbidden and disputes were settled by compulsory arbitration. These Fascist organizations were given the responsibility of submitting lists of parliamentary candidates to the Fascist Grand Council who then decided who should be allowed to stand. This structure took a long time to develop and was extremely inefficient. However, Mussolini

Mussolini arriving at the Vatican in Rome to meet Pope Pius XI in 1932.

Mussolini spent much money on new buildings and is seen here opening a Post Office in Rome, 1935.

managed to convince nearly everybody that it was superb. As the Minister of Education remarked in 1935, 'The Church, the king, the mob and the party were as convinced as he was that he (Mussolini) could make no mistakes.'

Although the Italian economy was still insecure, Mussolini managed to stabilize the value of the lire and tried to make Italy self-sufficient. For instance, in an effort to increase food production, he launched the 'Battle for Wheat'. One of his most successful schemes was the draining of the Pontine Marshes which had been a notorious breeding ground for the malaria-bearing mosquito. The marshes were reclaimed and turned into good agricultural land, on which a series of model towns and villages were built. Although such ventures had some success they did no more than scratch the surface of Italy's problems.

The new Roman Empire

Mussolini believed he was creating a new Roman Empire. He built monumental blocks of flats, railway stations and games stadia as well as a network of superb motorways called *autostrada*. Italy's hydroelectric resources were exploited and the railways were electrified. Not

31

The two dictators, Benito Mussolini and Adolf Hitler, meet in Germany in the 1930s.

satisfied with domestic triumphs, Mussolini turned to empire building. In 1935, he attacked Abyssinia (now Ethiopia). Between 1936 and 1939, he gave valuable help to General Franco in Spain. Worse still, he formed the Rome-Berlin Axis with Hitler in 1936, although he had at that time, no intention of becoming involved in a large-scale war. In 1939, he occupied Albania.

Mussolini boasted, 'My objective is simple. I want to make Italy great, respected and feared.' Envious of Hitler's successes in 1939–40, Mussolini declared war on France and Britain. By 1943, the new Roman Empire was in ruins and Mussolini was deposed by the Fascist Grand Council. Although he was 'rescued' by the Nazis and made the puppet leader of northern Italy, he was a mere shadow of his former self. In 1945, he was shot by Italian partisans and his corpse was strung up on telephone wires in the Grand Square in Milan. A critic had observed as early as 1919, 'He is a rabbit: a phenomenal rabbit: he roars. People who see him and do not know him mistake him for a lion.' Unfortunately, the majority of Italians did not discover this until too late.

5 FROM WEIMAR TO THE THIRD REICH

In the wake of German military defeat in 1918 came the November Revolution. Fritz Ebert, the leader of the Social Democrats, became the head of a provisional government. In December, this was challenged by the German Communists or Spartacists as they were called, led by Karl Liebknecht and Rosa Luxemburg. When civil war broke out, the provisional government called in the army to put the rising down. Liebknecht and Luxemburg were murdered by army officers.

The German people suffered terrible hardship and poverty as the result of the Allies' demands for reparations. Here Berliners search a rubbish dump for fuel.

In 1933 Hitler's Nazi Party was elected to the joy of some of the German people. This picture shows the celebrations of their Chancellor's victory in the Reichstag elections.

The Weimar Republic

A National Assembly met at Weimar in February 1919 and created a new constitution. Germany became a republic, headed by a president, who was elected by popular vote every seven years. He chose the cabinet and could in emergencies rule by decree. The new republican parliament consisted of two houses: the *Reichsrat* and the *Reichstag*. The *Reichsrat* represented the states or Lander and the *Reichstag* was elected by secret ballot and universal representation. On paper, Weimar Germany was a perfect democracy.

Crises

In its early years, the new state had to overcome a number of serious crises. In March 1920, some of the armed forces led by Dr Kapp and General von Luttwitz, tried to overthrow the republic. The ordinary people defeated this attempted revolution or *putsch* by striking until the rebels surrendered. Then, the Reparations Commission decided Germany should pay £100 million annually to compensate her enemies for all the losses they had incurred during the First World War. When Germany failed to meet these demands in 1923, the French occupied the great industrial area of the Ruhr. As a result, the German economy faltered, companies and banks collapsed and many people lost all their savings. The bitterness created by this incident provided fertile ground for Nazism to grow in.

The Beerhall Putsch

Adolf Hitler, the future leader of the Nazi movement, became a member of the National Socialist Workers Party in 1920 and quickly built up a large following by his attacks on the Socialists and Jews. He claimed they had caused Germany to lose the war by 'stabbing her in the back' and insisted that their policies were ruining the country. On 8 November 1923, Hitler tried to seize power in Munich, Bavaria. But when the police opened fire on a procession that he was leading in Munich, his followers fled. He was imprisoned and for a time the Nazi movement was powerless.

Return to affluence

This disastrous period was brought to an end by the rise to power of Gustav Stresemann who became Chancellor briefly in 1923 and remained Foreign Minister until his death in 1929. Under his influence, Germany gradually recovered. In 1924 and 1929, the reparations problem was partly solved by the Dawes and Young Plans. The French withdrew from the Ruhr and the German currency, the mark, was revalued. Germany joined the League of Nations in 1926 and signed the Kellogg-Briand Peace Pact in 1928.

Unfortunately, this new found stability and prosperity was brought to an end by the collapse of the New York Stock Market, the Wall Street Crash. The German economy disintegrated and unemployment increased at an alarming rate: there were 1,320,000 unemployed in 1929, 3,000,000 in 1930, 4,350,000 in 1931, 5,100,000 in 1932 and 6,000,000 in 1933. As the number of jobless rose, the popularity of the Nazi Party soared. Hitler promised to solve Germany's problems by 'strong government'. Gradually, with the help of Hermann Goering, his second-in-command and an ex-fighter plane ace, he won the support of many of the most important industrialists. The Nazis won twelve seats out of 647 in the *Reichstag* in 1929, 107 in 1930, 230 in the first election in 1932 and 196 in the second.

The Enabling Law

Although President Hindenburg deeply distrusted Hitler, he was persuaded to offer him the chancellorship in 1933. When the *Reichstag* building was burnt down shortly afterwards, Hitler blamed the Communists and had them excluded from parliament. In the ensuing election, the Nazis obtained an overall majority and on 22 March 1933, Hitler passed the Enabling Law which gave him dictatorial powers. With startling rapidity, Hitler 'Nazified' Germany. All the State governments were abolished and their powers transferred to the central government. The independent trade unions were closed down and replaced by the Nazi Labour Front. All political parties apart from the Nazis were abolished. Any opposition was smashed into silence by the S.A., the Nazi militia, and the S.S., the infamous state police. In 1934, hundreds of Hitler's political enemies were killed during the 'Night of the Long Knives'. Less dangerous opponents were locked up in concentration camps. Hitler boasted, 'I have burned out democracy and set authority in its place.'

Anti-Semitism

Hitler then turned on the Jews. In 1935, he passed the Nuremburg Laws which declared, 'A Jew cannot be a citizen of the *Reich* (the German State). He cannot exercise the right to vote; he cannot occupy public office ... Any marriages between Jews and citizens of German or kindred blood are herewith forbidden.'

The Jews were stripped of their rights as citizens of the Third Reich as Hitler intended to breed a master race: 'Every Aryan hero should marry a blonde Aryan woman with blue, wide-open eyes, a long oval face, a pink and white skin, a narrow nose and a small mouth.' The children of these perfect specimens were to occupy large areas of Europe, once their inferior inhabitants like the Slavs had been exterminated. This was why Hitler demanded *lebensraum* (living space) for the German people.

Nazi propaganda

By creating the Hitler Youth, the Führer (German for 'the leader' as Hitler was called) 'captured the children heart and soul.' There were six million members. The schools and universities became vehicles for political education. Josef Goebbels headed the State Propaganda Ministry and censored newspapers, books, films and the radio. The Nazis created hugely impressive spectacles for the ordinary people to

The burning of the Reichstag building in 1933 was blamed on the Communists.

A 1934 German poster depicts a pure 'Aryan' German woman regarding Hitler as the saviour of her country.

Some of the six million members of the Hitler Youth.

enjoy, like the rally described below:

> The immense building was well lighted and hung with the familiar scarlet flag, whose black swastika stands out startlingly from a circular white ground. Huge slogans covered the walls . . . While the crowds still continued to arrive, the Nazi bands played military music . . . The Leader comes. Preceded by flags, he paces between two lines of his Storm Detachments. The entire multitude leaps to its feet, and one shout breaks, again and yet again, from 125,000 throats; Heil Hitler. The roar continues till he has shaken hands on the platform; a hush falls . . . The Leader raises his hand and speaks. For three-quarters of an hour no pin fell, no single person coughed, so absolute was the spell.

Hitler also silenced the churches. In 1933, he signed a concordat or agreement with the Pope. His ally, Pastor Ludwig Muller, became the Evangelical (Protestant) Bishop of the German Reich.

The Four Year Plan

Hitler was determined to make Germany self-sufficient. In 1936, Goering introduced a Four Year Plan. This was to make Germany independent of imported raw materials and goods, by setting up their own new industries to produce among other things, synthetic materials. Food prices and rents were controlled. The slums were cleared and the country criss-crossed by superb motorways called *autobahnen*. These economic policies were preparations for war. Rearmament began and in March 1935 conscription was reintroduced.

Although many Germans had serious doubts about Hitler and the Nazis, most felt that they had given Germany back her pride and had won the respect of other nations. However, this did not mean they wanted war. But it was war for which the Nazis were preparing.

Hitler and the Nazis were preparing for war in 1935 as the launching of these new U-boats at Kiel demonstrates.

6 THE RUSSIA OF LENIN AND STALIN

Russia was the most backward country in Europe. It suffered severely during the First World War when few services were available even for casualties: 'Freight trains came into Moscow, in which the wounded lay without straw, often without clothing, badly bandaged and unfed for several days.' The communications system broke down and the towns were desperately short of food and fuel. When the people of Petrograd, the capital, rose in revolt in February 1917, the Empress completely underestimated the danger: 'Young people run and shout that there is no bread, simply to create excitement.' A few days later, the emperor was forced to abdicate and a provisional government was set up.

The provisional government

The provisional government failed to satisfy the people's needs for food, higher wages and peace. In June 1917, the Russian army made one final assault on the German forces and was horribly defeated. The ordinary people in Petrograd rose in revolt when they heard the news, but the July Revolution was put down by the Petrograd garrison.

A gun-battle in the streets during the revolution in Petrograd in 1917.

When it became known that Lenin and the Bolsheviks wanted to overthrow the provisional government, General Kornilov tried to seize power, declaring 'It's time to hang the German supporters and spies with Lenin at their head.' His troops, however, deserted him and in October, the Bolsheviks seized power in Petrograd, Moscow and many other Russian towns. Lenin announced, 'We shall now proceed to construct the socialist order.' The land, industry, the banks and the communications system were nationalized and run by the workers. Marriage was abolished and education made available for everyone. People of any race, religion and class were declared equal.

The Civil War

Civil war broke out almost immediately between the Reds (the Bolsheviks) and the Whites (the Monarchists). Lenin ordered: 'All those against the revolution, all spies, ruffians, hooligans etc. (are) to be shot by the *Cheka*' (the secret police). Both sides used the utmost brutality, but the Whites were the most hated as they were in league with the British, Americans and Japanese, who had invaded Russia hoping that the revolutionaries would be defeated. As famine spread among the townspeople, Lenin sent out bands of Red Guards led by political officers called commissars to force the peasants to hand over their food supplies: 'savage peasants would slit open a commissar's belly, pack it with grain, and leave him by the roadside as a lesson to all.'

Permanent Revolution

By 1921, the Whites were in full retreat and the Red Army invaded Poland. For a time all Europe quaked in fear until the Reds were defeated at the Battle of the Vistula and had to make peace. However, Lenin, Trotsky and most of the other Bolshevik leaders believed in 'permanent revolution': that to be successful the revolution had to spread from Russia to the rest of the world. For the time being Russia was exhausted and so Lenin introduced the New Economic Policy which stimulated the economy by denationalizing small industries and allowing the peasants to sell their crops. This was only a temporary measure. Lenin intended to continue 'the march to Socialism' as soon as the economy was strong enough.

By this time, there were ominous signs that Russia was becoming a one-party dictatorship. When the Socialist sailors of Kronstadt (just outside Petrograd), rose in revolt demanding that the Soviets (the local assemblies) of workers, soldiers and sailors be consulted, they were executed. Shortly afterwards, Lenin suffered the first of a series of strokes which led to his death in January 1924. Lenin had hoped that Trotsky would replace him, but he, too, was ill and Josef Stalin, the Man of Steel, wormed his way to power by playing off one Bolshevik

Lenin was the founder of Bolshevik Communism. An attempt to assassinate him in 1918 and a series of strokes led to his death in 1924.

Attrocities took place on both sides during the civil war between Bolsheviks and Whites.

leader against another. Trotsky was stripped of power and driven into exile and the other Bolshevik leaders were eliminated one by one.

Socialism in one country

Once firmly established in power, Stalin set about creating 'Socialism in one country'. His idea was to make Russia a model Communist State so that people everywhere would want to follow its lead. Stalin started the process by introducing the first Five Year Plan which called for 'collectivization' and 'industrialization'. Stalin believed that Russia would never be able to grow enough food until the peasants were forced to unite their holdings in great collective or State farms. When the better-off peasants, the Kulaks, refused, Stalin announced, 'We must annihilate them as a social class.' As a result, 'trainloads of dispossessed peasants left for the icy north ... old folk starved to death in mid-journey, new-born babies were buried beside the roadside.' Eventually, this brutal policy succeeded and helped Stalin finance 'industrialization'.

Between 1928 and 1932, Stalin concentrated on developing Russia's heavy industry: the production of coal, iron and steel was greatly increased. Although harsh methods were employed, many people believed in the new Russia. As an American reported, 'Tens of thousands of people were enduring the most intense hardships and many of them did it willingly and with boundless enthusiasm.' This was partly the consequence of the 'endless outpour and downpour of propaganda.' There was strict censorship of newspapers, books, films and the radio. 'What is demanded of the artist,' a French visitor remarked, 'is that he shall conform.' Failure to conform resulted in severe punishment.

The new society

Lenin had promised that the new Russia would be an egalitarian society. But as a commentator remarked, 'membership of the Communist party means that one belongs to a privileged class (with) country homes, the best housing and similar things.' Nevertheless, some important steps were taken to improve conditions in Russia. More schools

Following Lenin's death Stalin came to power and introduced collective farming.

were built although Stalin also reintroduced school fees. He like Lenin placed great emphasis upon the youth movement, the Pioneers and the *Komsomol*, which provided political education as well as recreational pursuits. Soviet women were treated as equals and were able to follow uninterrupted careers as crèches and kindergarten were provided for very young children. Although the State medical service was a disgrace when Stalin came to power, he gradually improved its quality by building new hospitals and giving priority to the training of doctors. Stalin disapproved of the so-called 'sexual revolution' and discouraged divorce and birth control. The main disadvantage of Stalin's policies was the brutality with which they were carried out. He insisted that everything be done at break-neck speed because he feared that enemies inside and outside of Russia were determined to overthrow him.

Fighting barbarism with barbarism
In 1934, Stalin made use of the murder of one of his henchmen, Kirov, to purge the Communist party. The old Bolshevik leaders were arrested, tortured and forced to make false confessions. A series of 'show trials' took place in 1936, 1937 and 1938, in which leader after

Between 1928 and 1932 Stalin developed Russia's steel and other heavy industries.

46

Stalin was a very ruthless man who played a great part in the modernization of Russia.

leader admitted plotting against Stalin before being condemned and executed. In all, well over a million members of the Communist party were executed or sent to the labour camps. Such was their belief in Communism that some wrote 'long live Stalin' with their own blood. Not even the army escaped the 'Great Purge'. Marshal Tukachevsky, the hero of the Civil War, was 'eliminated' as were thousands of other officers on false evidence provided by the Nazi Gestapo. *Pravda*, the State newspaper, described them as 'Spies, despicable hirelings of Fascism, traitors to their country' and demanded 'Shoot them'. The purges only ceased with the outbreak of the Second World War.

Although Stalin was a monstrously brutal dictator, his achievements were many and great. As one of his successors grudgingly admitted, 'Like Peter the Great, Stalin fought barbarism with barbarism, but he was a great man.'

7 NORMALCY TO THE NEW DEAL

The United States emerged from the First World War the greatest power in the world. Woodrow Wilson, her President and a Democrat, hoped to produce a better world and worked hard to make the peace treaties fair and to set up the League of Nations. Unfortunately, Congress, the American parliament, had no such beliefs and the Senate rejected the Treaty of Versailles just after the President had been incapacitated by a stroke. The United States decided to isolate herself from the rest of the world.

The Jazz Age

A Republican, Warren Harding, won the presidential election of 1920. His victory was not so much 'a landslide, it was an earthquake'. The twenties were the age of prohibition, when the sale of alcohol was forbidden and 'speakeasies', illegal drinking houses, appeared everywhere. Racism was rampant. The Ku Klux Klan, a fanatical racist society of white southerners, openly attacked blacks; 'Lynchings increased from thirty-four in 1917 to sixty in 1918 and to more than seventy in 1919 ... fourteen negroes were burned publicly.' In 1919, 'mobs roamed the slum areas of the city (Chicago) for thirteen days, burning, pillaging and killing with the National Guard unable to subdue them.' The political persecution of suspected 'Reds' (Communists) was just as vicious. 'Without warrants for arrest, men were carried off to police stations (and) subjected there to secret inquisitions commonly known as the "third degree".'

Scandals and Normalcy

Although Harding was a well-intentioned man, many of his friends were corrupt. The Secretary of the Interior, for instance, was detected selling off to the highest bidders the State oil reserves at Elk Hills and Teapot Dome. In April 1923, however, Harding died of a heart attack and was succeeded by Calvin Coolidge, a simple, religious man, who was determined to restore 'normalcy', by which he meant prosperity. During his presidency, industry boomed. Henry Ford, the motor car manufacturer, introduced assembly-line production. By 1929, the United States was manufacturing twenty-six and a half million cars a year. America was the envy of the world with its chain stores and

Americans drinking in an illegal drinking house known as a 'speakeasy'. This was the age of prohibition when the sale of alcohol was forbidden.

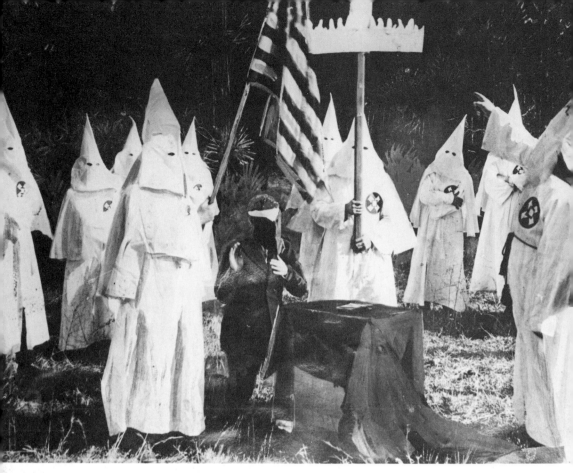

A meeting of the Ku Klux Klan, a fanatical racist society of white southerners, which was rampant in the 1920s.

vast array of consumer goods such as vacuum cleaners, washing machines and refrigerators. Taxes and prices were low. Although a few thousand Americans made enormous fortunes, millions lived in poverty. This gross inequality in the distribution of wealth threatened the American economy. In spite of the boom, some industries like agriculture suffered throughout the period.

The Wall Street Crash

Herbert Hoover, another Republican, succeeded Coolidge in 1928, declaring, 'We in America today are nearer to the final triumph over poverty than ever before in the history of any land.' For a time, the boom continued, but then on 23 October 1929 speculators on the Wall Street stock exchange started to sell off their shares. Next day, '12,894,650 shares changed hands, many of them at prices which shattered the dreams and the hopes of those who had earned them.' Things were so bad that a humourist joked, 'You had to stand in line to get a window to jump out of.'

At first Hoover believed he could solve the problem by behaving as if nothing had happened. Although many politicians called on him to increase unemployment benefits for the millions of jobless and to create jobs by public expenditure, he refused. Eventually, he set up a Reconstruction Finance Corporation. This lent money to big companies but did nothing to deal with the real problems. 'Long queues formed in front of the places where charitable institutions handed out food, these were the breadlines. ... In the streets of New York, there were hordes of men to be seen, each standing by a basket of apples, sadly repeating, "Buy an apple ... buy an apple".'

The New Deal
When Hoover's period of office ended in 1932, the United States was still deep in the grip of the Depression. At last, the Democrats found a dynamic presidential candidate in Franklin Delano Roosevelt. He oozed optimism demanding 'bold and persistent experimentation' and announcing, 'The only thing we have to fear is fear.' Roosevelt swept

Model T Fords arranged for delivery after leaving the assembly line.

to power and declared, 'I pledge you, I pledge myself, to a new deal for the American people.'

Roosevelt had no plans for a programme of legislation, but quickly set up 'a brains trust' to advise him. In 1933, bill after bill was rushed through Congress with hardly a pause. A civilian corps of a quarter of a million young men was set to work planting trees, building dams and draining marshes. By the Agricultural Adjustment Act, the Government took over the farmers' mortgages. Three and a half million dollars were allocated to public works which provided millions of new jobs. At the same time working conditions were improved by the National Industrial Recovery Act: working hours were cut, minimum wage rates set, excessive competition prevented and collective bargaining agreed. 'The New Deal', Roosevelt vowed 'seeks to cement our society, rich and poor, manual worker and brain worker, into a voluntary brotherhood of free men, standing together, striving together, for the common good of all.'

Worried New Yorkers gather outside the stock exchange during the Wall Street Crash in 1929.

A scene on a New York street following the Wall Street Crash.

Roosevelt was elected President of the United States four times.

Opposition grows

Roosevelt's political opponents feared that he was trying to make himself a dictator. Then, the Supreme Court declared the National Industrial Recovery Act and the Agricultural Adjustment Act unconstitutional. Roosevelt was forced to attack: 'We have witnessed the domination of government by financial and industrial groups, numerically small but politically dominant.' In 1936, he introduced a new scheme for social security, unemployment and old age benefits and another for slum clearance and the encouragement of home-buyers.

During the 1936 presidential election campaign, Roosevelt took his stand on 'Protection of the family and the home; establishment of a democracy of opportunity for all people; and aid to those overtaken by disaster', and won the greatest victory in American political history. This however was the turning point in his fortunes. From then on he encountered more difficulties with Congress which, for instance, rejected a plan for a huge public works programme in 1939. His reform programme slowed down and there were still nine million unemployed when the Second World War broke out.

Pearl Harbor

Although Roosevelt sympathized with the Allies, he had to proceed with the utmost caution as most Americans wanted the United States to have nothing to do with the war. In spite of claims that he was a warmonger, Roosevelt fought his Republican opponent, Wendell Wilkie, to a standstill in the 1940 presidential election campaign. Although he was elected for a third term, his majority was halved. Roosevelt helped the Allies by his Lend-Lease arrangements which enabled the British, for example, to obtain replacement shipping for the vessels sunk by Nazi submarines. Then, in December 1941, the Japanese bombed the American Pacific Fleet in Pearl Harbor and the United States declared war on Japan. Shortly afterwards, Hitler proclaimed war on the United States and America found herself fighting on a multitude of different fronts.

Roosevelt proved to be as effective a wartime as a peacetime leader. In 1944, he was re-elected for a record-breaking fourth term even though his health had deteriorated under the heavy strain of his long period in power. When he died on 12 April 1945, the Allies were in sight of victory.

The bombing of Pearl Harbor in December 1941 brought the United States into the Second World War.

8 COUNTDOWN TO WAR

At the height of the Great Depression in 1932–3, the peacemakers held a Disarmament Conference at Geneva. Hitler's rise to power in 1933 ended whatever slight chance of success it had. At first, he announced, 'Germany is at any time willing to undertake further (disarmament) obligations in regard to international security if all other nations are ready to do the same.' In October 1933, however, Germany withdrew from the League of Nations.

Nazi Germany accepted

In face of potential danger of a rejuvenated Germany, the French and Russians formed the Franco-Russian Pact and agreed to come to each other's aid in the case of an unprovoked attack. Even though this was aimed at Germany, Stalin and Hitler were already conducting secret negotiations. In fact Stalin was able to purge the Russian army's officer corps with the help of the Gestapo (the Nazi secret political police).

Even though Hitler was involved in the murder of Dollfuss, the Austrian Chancellor, in 1934, the powers were still prepared to make deals with him. In January, the Nazis and the Poles signed a non-aggression pact which contained secret clauses enabling the Germans

In 1933 the German delegation (pictured here) withdrew from the League of Nations.

German troops reoccupy the demilitarized Rhinelands in 1936.

to train pilots for their *Luftwaffe* (air force) and tank commanders for their Panzer regiments in Poland. In July, Britain and Germany arranged the Anglo-German Naval Agreement by which the Nazis agreed to content themselves with a navy thirty-five per cent of the size of Britain's. This was in direct contravention of the Treaty of Versailles. As a result, the Germans built a superb fleet of 'pocket' battleships and cruisers with 'British support'. These vessels were to do great damage to Allied shipping during the Second World War.

Rearmament

The Saarlanders, who had been under League of Nations' protection, voted to join the Third Reich in 1935. This demonstration of support encouraged Hitler to refuse to accept the armaments clauses of the Treaty of Versailles. This frightened Britain, France and Fascist Italy into setting up the Stresa Front by which they guaranteed Germany's existing frontiers. The Front's unity collapsed later in the year, however, when the Italians invaded Abyssinia, a fellow member of the League of Nations. Eden, a future British Foreign Secretary, called on the League to ban the sale of oil to Italy without success. Later, in 1938, Mussolini admitted to Hitler, 'If the League of Nations had followed Eden's advice, and had extended economic sanctions to oil, I would have had to withdraw from Abyssinia within a week.'

Appeasement

In 1936, to the consternation of his advisers, Hitler ordered German troops to occupy the demilitarized Rhinelands. The Nazi leader pointed out later, 'The forty-eight hours after the march into the Rhinelands were the most nerve-racking in my life. If the French had then marched

57

Neville Chamberlain visits Hitler in 1938.

into the Rhinelands, we would have had to withdraw with our tails between our legs.' Neither the French nor the British, however, did anything. Their leaders were shackled by memories of the terrible casualties suffered during the First World War. Chamberlain, the British Prime Minister, urged in 1938, 'We have to live with dictatorships ... We should take any and every opportunity to try to remove any genuine and legitimate grievance that may exist.' This was the so-called policy of appeasement for which the leaders of Britain and France have since been severely condemned.

Czechoslovakia betrayed
By this time, Hitler was sure of his destiny: 'neither threats nor warnings will move me from my path. I go with the assurance of a sleepwalker on the way which Providence dictates.' In 1938, he ordered his armies into Austria and carried out the *Anschluss* or union of the two countries. In the ensuing plebiscite (a vote of the entire nation), Hitler claimed that 99.05 per cent of the Austrian people voted for union. Hitler's eyes were already on Czechoslovakia which contained a discontented German minority. Chamberlain was determined to prevent war and arranged a series of summit meetings with Hitler at Berchtesgaden on 15 September, Godesburg on 22 September and finally at Munich on 29 September 1938. At the Munich Conference, the British and French leaders forced the Czechs to agree to Hitler's demands. As

a disapproving contemporary remarked, 'The partition of Czechoslovakia under pressure from England and France amounts to the complete surrender of the western democracies to the Nazi threat of force.'

The Sudetenlands containing the German minority was taken over in October 1938 and the rest of Czechoslovakia in 1939. Hitler was now uncontrollable. In March 1939, at the invitation of the local Nazi Party, he annexed the port of Memel in the Baltic state of Lithuania. In May, he signed the Pact of Steel with Mussolini, whose armies had just invaded Albania. In August, to the astonishment of the world, he signed the Nazi-Russian Pact. By this time, Hitler was convinced that the democracies would not dare to attempt to stop his expansion through Europe. Next, the city of Danzig was taken over and finally on 1 September 1939, the Nazis invaded Poland on the pretext that the Poles had attacked a German border radio station.

The outbreak of war

To Hitler's contemptuous surprise, Britain and France delivered an ultimatum, demanding the withdrawal of his troops from Poland. When he paid no attention, they declared war on 3 September. While the Nazi troops overran most of Poland, their Russian allies seized the rest, the Baltic States and Finland. While this was going on, there was almost no activity on the Western Front, the so-called 'Phoney War'. Then, in the spring of 1940, Nazi armies suddenly invaded

1 September 1939, the Nazis invade Poland.

France, Denmark and Norway. All three were easily subjugated in spite of British attempts to help. Mad with envy, Mussolini joined forces with Hitler in June hoping to obtain a share of the spoils. Shortly afterwards, the two dictators signed an Anti-Comintern (Communist) Pact with the Japanese who were conquering the Allies' colonies in the Far East.

The Battle of Britain

France fell to the well-organized German armies and the British Expeditionary Force escaped from Dunkirk after a terrible pounding. For a time, it seemed that Britain too would fall to the all-conquering Nazi armies. The German air force bombed Britain day and night in an effort to destroy national morale, but encountered far more vigorous opposition than they expected from the Royal Air Force, partially equipped with magnificient Spitfires and forewarned by a new radar system. Against all the odds, the 'Battle of Britain' was won

The end of appeasement. Britain and France declared war on Germany two days after the Germans invaded Poland.

London was heavily bombed during the Second World War. Here rescue teams search through the rubble for survivors.

by the defenders and the great German army that had been waiting to be transported across the Channel to Britain marched off in search of other prey. Britain had survived, but was weak and isolated.

Operation Barbarossa

Overcome with the belief in his destiny, Hitler ordered his forces to attack Soviet Russia. The unprepared Russian armies reeled back in confusion. By the onset of winter, German forces were besieging Leningrad, Moscow and Baku. In December 1941, the Japanese blundered by attacking the United States Pacific Fleet as it lay at anchor in Pearl Harbor. Shortly afterwards, Hitler declared war on America and for the second time in twenty-five years almost the whole world was engulfed by war. The Second World War raged until 1945 and in the process destroyed the uneasy world created by the peace treaties of 1919. A new world emerged in 1945 but with as many, if different problems from those that had tormented the period between 1918 and 1939.

9 CULTURE AND THE ARTS

The First World War had a profound effect on all classes and types of people including writers, composers and artists.

The age of the best seller

Between the wars, America produced a number of inspired writers. Many people thought Scott Fitzgerald gave the clearest picture of the new post-war age in *The Great Gatsby* (1925). Gatsby is a tycoon who believes in the good life and gives magnificent parties to impress Daisy Buchanan, a girl he had loved and lost. In 1929, Ernest Hemingway also achieved great success with *A Farewell to Arms*, the story of a love affair between an American officer and a British nurse in wartime Italy. From Germany came Remarque's masterpiece, *All Quiet on the Western Front* and from Britain, Richard Aldington's *Death of a Hero*. Throughout the inter-war period, many writers returned again and again to the horrors of war. T. H. White, for instance, produced an amusing story for children about King Arthur, called *The Sword in the Stone*. Later volumes in the same series called *The Once and Future King* became savage indictments of war.

The twenties and thirties were the age of the best seller. Most of these like Michael Arlen's *The Green Hat* are no longer read but they enjoyed enormous popularity at the time. Magazines of all kinds started to appear. Many like *Good Housekeeping* spread from America to Britain. Tabloid newspapers like the *Daily Mirror* and the *Graphic* also crossed the Atlantic and achieved great success in Britain. Children everywhere provided a flourishing market for 'comics' like *Chick's Own*, the *Rainbow* and *Tiger Tim's Weekly*. Many newspapers included comic strips like Rupert Bear in the *Daily Express*.

Politics and the Arts

Politics played their part in literature. Although Hitler's autobiography, *Mein Kampf* (My Struggle) received a poor reception everywhere but in Germany, Mussolini produced a novel which sold well and was translated into many different languages. One of his plays, *The Hundred Days*, was put on by the Old Vic in London. M. Deladier, the French Premier, published his finest speeches in a book called *The Defence of France*. Book Clubs did well. Gollancz's Left Book

62

Louis Armstrong was one of the great jazz players of the age.

The light music and dance tunes of the thirties mainly came from America.

Club in Britain had a membership of 50,000. Poets like Stephen Spender commented upon the plight of the unemployed:

> They lounge at corners of the street,
> And greet friends with a shrug of shoulder
> And turn their empty pockets out,
> The cynical gestures of the poor.

The Spanish Civil War awakened the consciences of people everywhere. The poet, W. H. Auden, asked:

> What's your proposal? To build the Just City?
> I agree. Or is it the suicide pact, the romantic
> Death? Very well, I accept, for
> I am your choice, your decision: yes, I am Spain.

Jazz, revue and popular songs

The twenties and thirties were also years of gaiety and laughter. 'Big Bands' toured America and Europe to rapturous applause. America gave Europe jazz and young people enthused over the playing of Louis Armstrong, Pee Wee Russell, Bix Beiderbecke, Benny Goodman and Duke Ellington. All kinds of new dances like the Charleston and Black

Bottom were the rage. Revue was at its peak with shows like Gershwin's *Funny Face* and Noel Coward's *On With The Dance*. Everybody hummed the popular songs of the day like:

> Just Molly and me
> And Baby makes three—
> We're happy in My Blue Heaven.

The Pictures

In the twenties, silent films were still at their peak with stars like Rudolph Valentino and Douglas Fairbanks. When Valentino suddenly died 'a number of girls committed suicide and indescribable scenes took place at his funeral.' Of Douglas Fairbanks, it was said: 'There was no man in the audience who hesitated to identify himself with this knight of the screen, escaping from his humdrum life into gallant adventures.' In 1929, Al Jolson starred in the first 'Talkie' *The Jazz Singer* and a new flood of Hollywood stars achieved world-wide fame. Going to the 'pictures' became part of most people's lives. Every European country produced great directors: in France, Renoir, Cocteau

A Charleston competition under way in New York in 1926.

In the twenties silent movies were at their peak. This shows Rudolph Valentino on a film set at Paramount Studios.

and Clair; in Italy, de Sica and Rossellini; and in Russia, the great Eisenstein who produced *The Battleship Potemkin*, *Alexander Nevsky* and *Ivan the Terrible*.

The wireless

If most people went to the pictures at least once a week, they listened to the radio every day. The United States introduced the idea of 'sponsored programmes' with announcers reading advertising slogans during commercial breaks. Special brands of comedy and drama were produced for the 'wireless'. Soon, people were able to tune into broadcasting systems all over the world. In Britain, for example, many listeners enjoyed the music broadcast by the Bratislava station in Czechoslovakia. Radio was also an effective propaganda instrument and was used expertly in Fascist Italy, Nazi Germany and Soviet Russia. Even in the democracies, politicians had to learn how to 'perform' on the new medium. Television was just starting to make real headway when the Second World War broke out.

Art and architecture

The world of art was a bewildering mass of 'isms'. The Cubism of Cézanne and Picasso survived the First World War but was followed by Dadaism—'The Dadaist loves life', it was said, 'because he can throw it away every day.' In America, 'Realism' or the 'Ashcan (dustbin) School' reigned supreme for a time. After much experimentation, many artists gave up trying to paint reality and allowed their imaginations to run riot—these were the Surrealists led by Klee, Chirico and Dali.

An example of the Dadaist art movement by Hausmann.

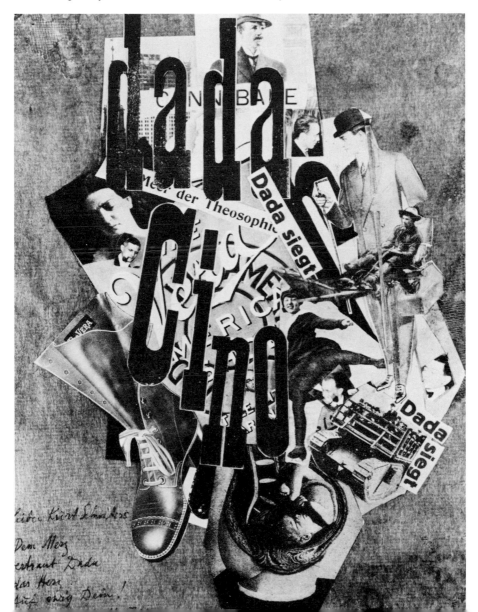

The legendary Australian cricketer, Don Bradman, batting.

For many architects, 'functionalism' was the order of the day. Walter Graupius and the Bauhaus school in Germany were the leaders in this field. They made great use of materials like concrete, steel and plate-glass to produce deceptively simple buildings. In America, the presiding genius was Frank Lloyd-Wright who created an apparently never-ending series of surprises. At Racine in Wisconsin, for example, he built an office block with walls made of brick and glass tubes and a interior supported by huge reinforced concrete pillars.

Sports
Sports of all kinds attracted enormous audiences. Wimbledon was dominated by the American Big Bill Tilden, the Frenchman Jean Borotra, the German von Kramm and the Englishman, Fred Perry. Boxing was dominated by black and white American boxers like Jack Dempsey

and Joe Louis, although the Frenchman, Georges Carpentier, and the Welshman, Tommy Farr, nearly staged surprises. While the cricketing world talked of the exploits of Jack Hobbs and the legendary Australian Don Bradman, America rang with praise of 'Babe' Ruth who took New York Yankees to the top of the baseball world. In golf, Bobby Jones and Walter Hagen ruled supreme. British football was dominated by Arsenal while Italy was the most successful international side, to Mussolini's undisguised delight.

The inter-war world was perfectly described by the British actor-playwright, Noel Coward; 'I knew that the world was full of hatred, envy, malice, cruelty, jealousy, unrequited love, murder, despair and destruction. I also knew, at the same time, that it was full of kindness, joy, pleasure, requited love, generosity, fur, excitement, laughter and friends.'

Britain's Fred Perry, became the first player to win the 'grand slam', the world's four major single titles in one year – Wimbledon, the U.S., French and Australian championships.

DATE CHART

1917
Feb–Mar   The Tsarist regime in Russia is overthrown.
Oct–Nov   The Russian Provisional Government is replaced by the Bolsheviks.

1918
11 Nov   The Germans are granted an armistice.

1919
The German Empire is divided up by the Great Powers as a result of the Treaty of Versailles. Mussolini forms the Fasci di Combattimento in Italy.

1920
Prohibition (the banning of the sale of alcoholic liquor) is introduced by the 18th Amendment to the American Constitution.

1921
Lenin introduces the New Economic Policy.

1922
'The March on Rome'—Mussolini becomes Prime Minister of Italy.

1923
The French occupy the Ruhr as the Germans are unable to pay their reparations in full.

1924
21 Jan   The death of Lenin leads to a struggle for power within the Bolshevik/Communist party in Russia. Ramsay Macdonald forms the first Labour Government in Britain's history. The Dawes plan reduces the size of the reparations which the Germans are required to pay the victorious Allies.

1924–26
The anti-black Ku Klux Klan is rampant in the south and midwest of America.

1928
Fifty-four nations sign the anti-war Kellogg-Briand Pact.

1929
23 Oct   Black Friday triggers the Wall Street Crash and the Great Depression. Stalin is recognised as the undisputed leader of Russia.

1931
A National Government is formed in Britain to deal with the economic crisis.

1933
Adolf Hitler becomes Chancel-

lor of Germany. Franklin D. Roosevelt is elected President of the United States and launches 'the New Deal'.

1934

'The Night of the Long Knives': Hitler has his main enemies murdered or taken to concentration camps.

1935

Hitler publishes the Nuremburg Laws stripping Jews of their rights as citizens of the Third Reich. The Italians invade Abyssinia, a member state of the League of Nations.

1936

'The Year of the Three Kings': George V dies, Edward VIII abdicates to marry Mrs Wallis Simpson and George VI succeeds to the throne.

1936–38

The Great Purge or *Chistka* of the Russian Communist Party.

1936–39

The Spanish Civil War between Socialists and Nationalists.

1938

13 Mar   Germany and Austria are united by the *Anschluss*.

29 Sep   The Munich Agreement by which the Sudetenlands in Czechoslovakia are ceded to Nazi Germany.

1939

22 May   Mussolini and Hitler sign the 'Pact of Steel'.

23 Aug   Stalin and Hitler agree the Russo-German non-aggression pact.

1 Sep   German forces invade Poland.

3 Sep   Britain and France declare war on Germany.

1941

7 Dec   The Japanese attack the American Pacific Fleet at Pearl Harbor without warning. The USA declares war on Japan; Germany declares war on the USA.

1942

Germany, Italy and Japan sign a full military alliance.

1943

July   Mussolini is dismissed from office and arrested.

1945

Franklin D. Roosevelt dies and is replaced by Harry Truman as President of the USA. Mussolini is murdered by Italian partisans while trying to escape to Germany. Hitler commits suicide rather than be captured by the Russian forces besieging Berlin.

7 May   The German armed-forces surrender unconditionally.

GLOSSARY

Abdicate   To renounce (a throne, power, responsibility).

Annihilate   To destroy completely.

Arbitration   The determining of a dispute by independent judges.

Anschluss   The union of Austria and Nazi Germany.

Bolsheviks   'The majorityites'; the members of the Russian Social Democratic party who eventually adopted the title the Communist party.

British Commonwealth of Nations   Those parts of the British Empire which had reached political maturity by the inter-war period: Australia, Canada, the Irish Free State, South Africa and New Zealand.

Cede   The transfer of lands by one country to another.

Communism   A political ideology or system which aims to bring about a society without social classes, in which private ownership is abolished and the means of production belong to the community as a whole.

Concentration camp   A guarded camp in which prisoners were held, under inhumane conditions.

Conscription   Compulsory military service.

Constitution   The method of ruling a country.

Demilitarization   The agreed exclusion of all armed forces from a specific area.

Democracies   Those countries which are governed by their elected representatives.

Depression   A particularly prolonged and deep slump involving a severe decline in trade and mass unemployment.

Dictator   A ruler who is not effectively restricted by a constitution or laws, a tyrannical ruler.

Diktat   A dictation—usually used with reference to the dictated Peace of Versailles.

Disarmament   The reduction of a country's stock of arms to the minimum needed for defence.

Egalitarian Society   One in which all the citizens are equal and there are no classes or orders of nobility.

Front   A French coalition or a major area of fighting during a war.

Garrison   Troops permanently stationed in a town to protect it and keep order.

Gold Standard   A legal obligation on the part of a country's central bank to sell gold at a fixed rate in terms of its national currency.

Kulaks   Prosperous Russian peasants who refused to have their land collectivized and were wiped out on Stalin's orders.

Left wing   The socialist side of politics.

Lock-out   To prevent (employees) from working during an industrial dispute, as by closing a factory.

Lynch   To kill (with a mob) a person for some supposed offence.

Masonic Movement   A number of secret orders or fraternities with special rites and ceremonies which trace their origins back to the Temple of Solomon–they were declared illegal by the Fascists.

Militia   A body of citizen (as opposed to professional) soldiers.

Minorities   Sizeable groups of people of a different nationality from the dominant group in a particular country.

Nationalists   Believers in the collection of all members of the same nation in one state OR people who believe that the interests of the state should take precedence over those of individuals.

Nazi   A member of the Nationalist Socialist German Workers' Party which seized power in Germany in 1933 under Adolf Hitler.

Neutralization   The exclusion by international law of armed forces from a specific area, e.g. the straits between the Black and Mediterranean Seas.

Non-Aggression Pact   An official treaty between two or more ex-enemies or potential enemies that they will not attack each other.

Partisans   'Amateur' freedom fighters.

Propaganda   Psychological means of persuading people to support a party or policy.

provisional government   A temporary government to rule until a general election provides a representative assembly.

Putsch   The violent overthrowing of a government.

Radar   Radio Detection and Ranging: the employment of reflected or retransmitted radio waves to locate objects.

Reichsrat   The council of representatives of state government within Germany from 1919–1934.

Reichstag   The sovereign assembly of the Weimar Republic (1919–33), also the building in Berlin in which this assembly met.

Reparations   Compensatory payments for damage done in war.

Right wing   The conservative side of politics.

Slogans   Phrases which sum up in a few words either a political policy or the advantages of a particular brand of produce.

Slump   A decline in trade, usually accompanied by a fall in prices and unemployment.

Socialism   The idea that the land, industry, banks, transport system etc. should be owned by the whole people instead of by individuals.

Soviet   A local committee or council of workers, peasants and soldiers to be found in Revolutionary Russia.

Totalitarian regime   A form of government where there is only one policy and one political party permitted, e.g. Communist Russia, Fascist Italy and Nazi Germany.

Third Reich   The Nazi dictatorship (1933–1945).

Treaties   Agreements between two or more countries.

Ultimatum   A final demand that a country carry out certain measures or the sender of the ultimatum will force that country to carry out the measures after a stated period of time.

Warmonger   A person who fosters warlike ideas or advocates war.

FURTHER READING

Absalom, R. N. L. *Mussolini and the Rise of Italian Fascism* Methuen, 1969

Bayne-Jardine, C. *Mussolini and Italy* Longman, 1966

Berwick, M. *The Third Reich* Wayland, 1971

Browne, H. *Hitler and the Rise of Nazism* Methuen, 1969

Elliott, B. J. *Hitler and Germany* Longman, 1966

Gibson, M. *Russia under Stalin* Wayland, 1979

Gregory, D. *Mussolini and the Fascist Era* Arnold, 1968

Hewison, A. R. C. *The Spanish Civil War* Arnold, 1969

Leeds, C. *Italy under Mussolini* Wayland, 1972

Parkinson, R. *Origins of World War Two* Wayland, 1970

Phillips, D. M. *Hitler and the Rise of the Nazis* Arnold, 1968

Roberts *Lenin and the Downfall of Tsarist Russia* Methuen, 1969

Roberts *Stalin: Man of Steel* Methuen

Snellgrove, L. E. *Franco and the Civil War* Longmans, 1965

Stacey, F. W. *Lenin and the Russian Revolutions* Arnold, 1968

Stacey, F. W. *Stalin and the Making of Modern Russia* Arnold, 1970

Yass, M. *The Great Depression* Wayland, 1973

INDEX

PICTURE ACKNOWLEDGEMENTS

The illustrations in this book were supplied by: BBC Hulton Picture Library 9, 11, 17, 28, 31, 41, 44, 50, 51, 52, 54, 58; Bridgeman Art Library cover; Imperial War Museum 32, 57; Mansell Collection 8, 14, 18; Museum of Modern Art, New York, 26 (Guernica painted by Pablo Picasso in 1937. Oil on canvas, 350 × 782 cm); Topham Picture Library 12, 13, 15, 19, 20, 21, 22, 23, 24, 25, 27, 30, 33, 34, 38, 40, 43, 45, 46, 55, 56, 59, 60, 61, 63, 64, 66, 67, 68, 69. The remaining pictures are from the Wayland Picture Library.